THE LOVE BOOK

The Love Book: Timeless Lessons on the Endless Love of the Lord

Copyright © 2020 The Jesus Center

ISBN: 9798657030099

A publication of Talll Pine Books

|| TALLPINEBOOKS.COM

*Printed in the United States of America

THE LOVE BOOK

Timeless Lessons on the Endless Love of the Lord

THEO KOULIANOS SR.

Tall Pine

My wife, Evelyn, and I dedicate this expression of God's love to Michael and Jessica's children: Theo Michael, Benny and Sofia; to Theo and Rachel's children: Theo Malachi, Henry and Caleb; and to Theo B. and Becky's children: Noah and Theo Jr.

Thank You, Lord, for such a beautiful inheritance. We love You, Lord, so much. Thanks for making a way that our family can ravish Your heart!

CONTENTS

A TESTIMONY OF GOD'S LOVE

As you begin reading *The Love Book*, I would like to share my true testimony of seeing the reality of the love of God. I could never adequately express it to you in words, yet I'll attempt to convey His love the best way I know how.

During my first trip to Brazil, I was with a Pastor Abraham and his brother-in-law, ministering in various cities near Sao Paulo. On our first day, the chief of police there invited us to minister to inmates within Brazil's largest federal prison. They asked us to minister and share Jesus with a section of prisoners, all former policeman who had succumbed to corruption and been found guilty of various crimes. I'll never forget the setting. The structure was poorly constructed. The roof, made of old, rusty corrugated tin, was riddled with holes. It was raining and the water was leaking through the tin roof. The walls had little paint remaining on them. The concrete floor was cold and damp. Some seventy-five inmates entered the room. As they came in, I saw desperation on their faces. My heart was moved. First, Pastor Abraham shared God's Word. Then it was time for me to minister. I began to reveal the love of Christ. I felt in my heart that the Holy Spirit wanted me to reveal just how deep, wide and incredible the love of God really is. In the middle of my ministering, my eyes became fixed on a man in the crowd. He was weeping, and I could sense fear all over him. I had no idea what it must have been like for him to go back to his cell and experience what he faced on a daily basis.

Prompted by the Spirit, I called the man forward. I happened to be wearing an expensive shirt but I felt God telling me to give it to this man. Friends, I cannot put in words how bad that room smelled. You could tell they had no regular access to a shower or any standard hygiene products. The man whom I had called forward wore an old t-shirt. More than likely, his shirt had not been washed in weeks or months. Caught up in the moment, I suddenly realized that I wasn't wearing an undershirt. There I was, standing before these men without a shirt on. After this man came forward, I asked him to take off his shirt and to put on my shirt. As he did so, an incredible smile came aCross his face. You could see just how good he felt about himself in that moment.

God then told me to put on his t-shirt—yes, that foul-smelling, dirty t-shirt. Reluctantly, I put it on. As I did, I began to weep. I started to sense in my heart the desperation of the love of Christ upon the Cross. He willingly made the greatest exchange in all of history, giving us His beautiful righteousness and taking our foulness and sin upon Himself. As I put on that man's shirt, I felt his pain and suffering, his filthiness and shame. I felt his desperation. At that moment, the prisoners stood up, weeping, and with their hands outstretched, praising God.

The love of God was revealed in such a glorious way that night that it marked my heart forever. I pray that as you read *The Love Book*, you too will have a similar spiritual experience. Perhaps one day, when you least expect it, God will have you do something that will demonstrate the depth of His love as well.

PREFACE

My hope and prayer is that, in reading *The Love Book*, the Holy Spirit will impart into your hearts the incredible gift of the love that our Father in Heaven has given to each of us. He gave His Son, as God's Lamb, to be slain on the altar of His Cross. Each of us, as well as all of mankind, were under the curse of sin. Each of us were condemned because of our guilt. Yet, out of His great love, God provided a sacrificial remedy to all who would receive His gift. What is that gift? It is the *Blood of the Lamb*, the only begotten Son of God—Jesus Christ of Nazareth. What can be more precious?

What could have greater value than God's gift to the world? Jesus said, in John 6:55, *"For my flesh is **real** food and my Blood is **real** drink"* (NIV, emphasis added). It is only by the Holy Spirit of God that we can come to know the gift of God by way of the Blood of His Son, Jesus. This gift of God's love is for *many*, not merely for a few. The Bible tells us that no man can receive the glory and honor for the sacrifice of this gift of love. The Blood of the Lamb belongs to you, to me, and to the entire world—to every sinful man, woman and child. This gift of love, flowing through the Blood of Christ, is for you and your family.

My hope is that you will believe in the Beloved Jesus, and that you shall be saved—both you and your household. Great joy awaits anyone who will stand, call on the name of the Lord Jesus Christ of Nazareth, and come to know the one true God, and Jesus, whom He sent. God bless you, and I thank you for taking the time to read *The Love Book.*

1

THE LOVE OF CHRIST URGES US ON

We must never forget the depths of the love of Jesus Christ of Nazareth, the Father and the Holy Spirit. The Father loved us so much that He did not withhold His own Son, as we learn in Romans 8:32. Jesus gave Himself *completely* for us. He did this to redeem us from everlasting death and to win back for us God's grace and our lost paradise—which is the Presence of the Lord.

The gospel of John famously states: *"The Word was made flesh, and dwelt among us"* (John 1:14). Philippians 2:7–8 talks of how Jesus emptied Himself, taking the form of a servant in this world and being obedient to the point of death. He subjected Himself to all the same miseries and struggles that man endures. Christ lowered Himself, taking on the form of a servant so He could become acquainted with our griefs and miseries. Not only did

Jesus accomplish these things for us, but Paul also writes:

> I am crucified with Christ: nevertheless I live; yet not I, but Christ liveth in me: and the life which I now live in the flesh I live by the faith of the Son of God, who loved me, and gave himself for me. (Galatians 2:20)

My faith in the Lord Jesus Christ is predicated on the fact that I know the depth of His love for me—that He gave Himself for me. There is no other love that is acceptable by God's standard. It is called *sacrificial love.* Jesus set the standard for that. Jesus is comprised of a love that is so overwhelming, He chose to live in affliction and contempt. He chose to die in bitterness on the Cross. Why would He do this? For one reason: to show us the love He bears for us. Christ loved us and gave Himself up for us.

This great love is a standard we can never attain in our own might. The bar is set so high that it requires God Himself to achieve it in us and through us. Therefore, it's not by our might or power but by the Spirit of God alone. He willingly gave Himself up to know the sorrow and the shame in a death more painful than anyone on earth will ever, or has ever, endured. It was for this reason that Paul wrote, *"The love of Christ urges us on"* (2 Corinthians 5:14 nrsv).

You must look into the heart of Paul to see the

objective of his call to the church. He is urging that everything we do for God be fueled by God's love. God's love is so powerful that it becomes the fuel that enables us to finish the race. God's overwhelming love in Paul's life urged him on, day after day, week after week, year after year—always pressing forward for the prize of the high calling.

So, I ask you, should not such a love place our hearts in a vise? Think of the divine vise in which we find our hearts. The love of Christ places our hearts in a divine vise of His beautiful, nail-scarred hands so that we can feel the force of His holy love. He is squeezing our love out of us and squeezing His love into us.

Let us cast ourselves on Jesus, who was crucified to die on the Cross. We must never let the Cross of Christ out of our heart's vision. We must always behold Jesus Christ, and Him crucified, because it speaks of His divine holy love. It is a love that Christ has for you. His love compels us to press forward and never to let go of Him. Let us die and rise with Him, that we might be consumed in the flames of His love. Jesus held nothing back from us, so we must hold nothing back of ourselves. Let me emphasize this clearly: *Jesus held nothing back of Himself from us.* He alone has the right to demand that we hold nothing of ourselves from Him. Let us live and let us die, by the Holy Spirit, in His loving arms each day.

There is no other way other than to deny

ourselves, take up our Cross daily and follow Him. Yet it's not merely a following based on a master/servant relationship. It's a following urged on by the *love* of Christ. Life or death cannot separate us from His love. Only the Holy Spirit can keep our hearts on fire with the *first love* of Jesus.

There was an early church song that went something like this: "Long live Jesus, whom I love. I love Jesus, who lives forever and ever." You can see the simplicity of their faith. Their bulwark and foundation was Jesus Christ and His love for His bride. Jesus has so great a love for us. His love made Him desire death on the Cross. The Cross was that place where He revealed His glorious affection for the whole world. What other way could He affirm the depth of His love than to suffer and to die upon the Cross, and to give up His Spirit as the final exclamation of His proclamation of love?

CHAPTER ONE

STUDY QUESTIONS

1) In what ways specifically has the love of Christ motivated you?

_____
_____
_____
_____
_____

2) What happens if we are fueled by things other than the love of Christ?

_____
_____
_____
_____
_____

3) Neither life nor death can separate us from the love of Christ. On a personal level, how does this impact your life today and in the future?

_____
_____
_____
_____
_____

Additional thoughts:

_____
_____
_____
_____
_____
_____
_____
_____
_____
_____
_____
_____
_____
_____

2

OH, LOVE

"Oh, love; oh, love." This was a cry of the early church saints whenever their eyes fixed upon the crucifix of our Lord. This too must be the cry of our hearts. How can our minds ever comprehend the great love of Christ that would compel Him to die on a Cross between two criminals? Some ask, "Why would such majesty and holiness submit to becoming such disgrace? Who was this Man that He would do such a thing?" To those questions, there is only one answer that will suffice: *love*. Love put aside dignity and self-respect. Love did not seek honor or acknowledgment. Love concerned Himself only with the dignity of His bride.

For this reason, only eyes of faith can see such love. The eternal Word literally became so zealous in His love for His creation that He put aside Himself. This is the mark of a true disciple of Jesus Christ—

that you put aside yourself for the love of God. It is said, "We see wisdom infatuated through the excess of love."

It was written that a woman of God took a wooden crucifix in her hands and cried out, "Yes, my Jesus; You are mad with love, my Jesus!" We can't possibly comprehend the love God has for us. Jesus is so in love with you that He went out of Himself for you. Each day of our lives, we must stop and ask the Holy Spirit to enable us to behold His Cross. With the eyes of our hearts, we must behold His love. As we celebrate Jesus' resurrection, we must fellowship with His sufferings. How can we not be set ablaze in our hearts at the sight of those flames of love in our Redeemer's heart, which was pierced by the lance of the Roman soldier?

What joy and happiness awaits us when we are burned by that same fire that burns in God for us! Only the Holy Spirit can do this. He is the One who enables us to know the incredible love of God. Jesus wants us bound to His love with Heavenly chains. An early church saint wrote, "The wounds of Jesus Christ cut through the most senseless hearts. They inflame the most frigid souls." Nothing pierces the heart of a non-believer like the wounds of Jesus Christ; from those wounds flows His love. Countless arrows of love flow from the heart of our Lord into ours, penetrating even the hardest of hearts. For by the Holy Spirit, He releases the arrows of love from our Lord into our hearts. When we speak of salvation, if the hard-hearted is singed by one of these flaming arrows of love from Christ's heart, they cannot remain the same. Therefore, we must encounter Jesus at the altar.

It is said, "The intensity of the flames of love that flows from the heart of our Lord will set afire the coldest soul. Out of His wounded side will come forth love that binds us with chains that the most rebellious heart cannot resist." All those who are lost need to be touched by the love of the gospel of Jesus Christ—touched by the love of the Cross, by the Blood of the Cross. To those who have been called to preach the gospel, you have been gifted to the church and you must always speak of His love. It must be clear in every sermon. This is a love that will compel contrition and repentance. Jesus Christ is your Redeemer. He has loved you in such a way that anyone who reflects upon His love will do nothing but love Him back and call upon His name. *What must I do to be saved?"* was the desperate inquiry of the jailer in Acts 16:30. Paul, compelled by the love of Christ, urged this man who had locked him up to have faith in Jesus.

But that the world may know that I love the Father; and as the Father gave me commandment, even so I do. Let us rise and be on our way. (John 14:31 paraphrased)

When Jesus said, "Let us rise and be on our way,"

what was He referring to? The answer is clear: we all must die upon the Cross. Jesus Christ died upon His Cross for all mankind. This was His *way*. The way of Jesus Christ is the way of love. It is paid with the Blood of His Cross. So, I ask, can any of us ever understand just how intensely the love in Jesus' heart burns? It is said that He was commanded to suffer and to die. But I tell you, it has been written, "Had He been commanded to die one thousand times, He would have willingly done so." That's how much Jesus loves you. That's how much He loves the world.

The gospel declares that Jesus hung on the Cross for three hours. But if it had been necessary for Jesus to hang there until Judgment Day, He would have done so. That's the depth of His love; Jesus loves us enough to suffer for us. His love is greater than suffering. The greatest sign of the greatest love was found in Jesus as He laid down His life for His friends. He loved us and proved it with every wound and bruise upon His body. He proved it with the spikes that were driven into His hands and with every lash to His back. When we truly know of His holy love, we will forever be amazed. There's a burning sensation that will cut to the very depth of your soul.

Thus, I ask, how could anyone of us betray such a love? Once we have been burned by the flames of His love, we cannot backslide. You cannot backslide if you apprehend the love of Christ in your heart.

You cannot backslide, for you will live with the fear of God and His first love.

Look at the apostolic fathers such as Ignatius. He was the bishop of Antioch, discipled by the apostle John. When Ignatius, a man in his eighties, refused to deny Christ and was thrown to the lions in a Roman arena, he begged no one to save him from the mouth of the beasts. This is what he wrote before his death: "Allow me to become food for the wild beasts, through whose instrumentality it will be granted me to attain to God. I am the wheat of God, and let me be ground by the teeth of the wild beasts, that I may be found the pure bread of Christ. ...Then shall I truly be a disciple of Christ."

Ignatius received a love from Christ and returned that love to Christ, which enabled him to face the harshest of realities and to gladly suffer for the cause of the gospel. He was forced to walk on burning coals and even yearned for the torment, that he might glorify the Son and the love that He had for our Master. These saints rejoice in what the world dreaded.

We must apprehend His love, that we too may embrace what the world hates. It is written that the soul married to Jesus Christ upon the Cross thinks nothing is more glorious than to bear the marks of the crucified One, Jesus Christ of Nazareth. We must ask of the Lord, "How can I repay You, Lord? For

Your love and Blood do not deserve to be recompensed with our Blood."

By faith, we must set our hearts in His Blood and be nailed to His Cross, that we too may cry, "It is not I who live but Christ who lives in me." (See Galatians 2:20.) We must declare to the world, "We are crucified in Christ." By the empowerment of the Holy Spirit, in our hearts, we must daily be nailed to the Cross of Christ. It is the place of love. It is said, "We must cry out, even to the crown of thorns that was upon our Master's head, that somehow, those thorns would be made wider so that we too may place ourselves under His crown." Only with our Master is such love and power to be found.

CHAPTER TWO
STUDY QUESTIONS

1) The chapter describes a deep, intimate love for Jesus. How can we cultivate this? What does bridal love look like practically?

_____
_____
_____
_____
_____

2) Have you ever truly cried out to God with a heart of love? What was the result? Did God encounter and/or speak to you?

_____
_____
_____
_____
_____

3) The chapter speaks of our need to die upon the Cross. What does this mean? What are the effects of not dying daily and how does this neglect impact our lives as believers?

_____
_____
_____
_____
_____

Additional thoughts:

_____

_____

_____

_____

_____

_____

_____

_____

_____

_____

_____

_____

_____

_____

3

INTIMACY'S BLESSING

There is a blessing found in our intimacy with Jesus Christ. In my heart, I would say that the greatest blessing of God is the blessing of Jesus Himself and His Presence. When we look at our souls, we speak of our mind, will, emotions and intellect. Our souls are meant to be flooded and set aflame with the *first love* of Jesus Christ. The very thought of God is to bring a burning flame of love into our souls. God is longing that the fire of His love would burn within our hearts, that all the world would be set ablaze with first love for Christ.

It's as though we are to be bathed in the glory and the love of our Beloved Jesus. Our desire should be the desire what David displayed when he cried out, *"One thing have I desired of the Lord, that will I seek after; that I may dwell in the house of the Lord all the days of my life, to behold the beauty of the Lord, and to enquire in his temple"* (Psalm 27: 4). Each man, woman and child have a desperate need for the Presence of Jesus. In His Presence, we behold His beauty and are enraptured in His love. In this place, our hearts are branded, as we behold Him face to face. The more our souls are flooded with the Presence of God, the more our souls are saturated with the Lordship of the Holy Spirit. The more intimacy with Jesus we experience, the more we will realize the great abundance of His glory and love.

The depths of the living waters of the glory of God flow into the soul that is surrendered, broken and contrite. God wants us to crave the Presence of His Son. He wants our hearts flooded with a desire that is so deep, it cannot be explained, a desire for an ever deepening intimacy with Jesus, who proclaimed, "If anyone is thirsty, let him come to Me and drink." (See John 7:37.) You see, only the thirsty come to Jesus. He went on to say, "Whoever believes in me, as the Scripture has said, streams of living water will flow from within him." (See verse 38.) By this, He meant the Spirit, whom those who believed in Him would later receive. Until that time, the Spirit had not been given, since Jesus had not yet been glorified. I pray that every reader of this book will comprehend in their hearts that Jesus is the Son of God. He is the Beloved of our hearts. He will rise up in our hearts as we thirst for Him in humility and brokenness of heart.

God's rivers of living water flow in those who believe in Him. The Greek word is *bēstevo*, which means to trust in Him totally and to submit to Him with total reliance. These divine rivers of living water that God longs to flow through us are not available to those who half-heartedly submit to Him. Only the Holy Spirit can inspire, incite, and fan the flame that takes us, by faith, into His Presence with *cords of love*.

Jesus is faith. And when our lives are fanned with this love and adoration in the Presence of God, His Presence will become more and more revealed each time we are in His Presence. Every time we fan the flame of love by faith, the glory of the Lord's Presence is revealed. The Holy Spirit is, quite literally, the God who imparts the glory of Jesus. Only God can reveal God. The Holy Spirit tears apart the veil of our flesh and empowers us to stand before God, burning with desire.

He wants all of you. As Thomas à Kempis wrote, "Everything for everything." God wants everything, for He gave everything. He wants all of you, every day. He longs to see you, more and more, the denial of self. It's a matter of taking up your Cross daily, following Him, adoring Him, and praising Him. Worship like this fans the flame in your heart, greater and greater. As a result, the Spirit of God will draw you into a deeper encounter with Himself. Every encounter with God allows you to communicate with Him and to commune with Him. As you do, He will reveal more and more of Himself and of the Lord Jesus Christ.

The Holy Spirit, the *flame of love*, is the Spirit of the Bridegroom. The *flame of love* is the Spirit of Jesus Christ, our first love. Our souls cannot be constrained. Our souls shall know Him. Our hearts will burn for Him and we shall be consumed in His love. He transforms us into the image of Christ Jesus. This flame of love, the Holy Spirit, continues to burn, flaring up within us every moment of every day. We must only be hungry and thirsty for Him.

Every time the Holy Spirit reveals Christ to our hearts, our souls are saturated with His love. The more the Spirit of God burns within us, the more we will encounter His Presence and the more we will become refreshed in His divine holiness, for there is a refreshing in the Presence of God. It is in that place that our souls are truly conformed. It's only in the Beloved's Presence that we are conformed and given the mind of Christ. The more you long, hunger, thirst, and cry out, the more the Holy Spirit works within you. The flames of the Holy Spirit will rise and burn, consuming more and more of your soul.

Every flame is as an arrow, shot from the quiver of the Lord's heart. It's an arrow of His love that pierces our hearts and sets them intensely aflame. He is piercing our hearts with his arrows of love. Many ask, "What is true *first love?*" To adequately discover this answer, we must realize that it's critical for the flame of Christ's love to be continually fanned into a blazing fire in our hearts. When we speak of first love, we are speaking of the soul's desire to unite and become one with the heart of Christ. It is a desperate life of love within our hearts. Such a love is so precious to Jesus. A lifetime of doing good deeds cannot compare with the first love for our Beloved.

There's one thing God wants us to crave from Him. There's one thing He wants us to seek above all else: *to abide in the living Presence of Jesus.* His sacrificial love on the Cross has gained us the privilege of dwelling in and with Him. His house is far more than a tabernacle made with man's hands. His tabernacle is His heart. In His heart, we are to dwell and find His sweetness and rest. This is God's ultimate desire for us.

As we cry out with hunger and thirst for Jesus, He will instill within us a strong desire to live life as close to Him as possible. It's only by God that we want God and remain with God. He takes pleasure in our intimacy with Him. He takes pleasure in our worship. He takes pleasure in our prayers. Jesus is our Shelter in the good and the bad. The Bible says He is our Shelter in the time of trouble. (See Psalm 46:1.) This is where we need to be found. When the times of trouble come, we are to be found in His Presence, for in His Presence, we are hidden. It is in this holy place that He gathers us, as a mother hen gathers her chicks to her heart. When God gathers us, He embraces and protects us in His love.

CHAPTER THREE
STUDY QUESTIONS

1) The chapter highlights our need for true intimacy with Jesus. Why does such a posture position us to receive from Jesus?

_____
_____
_____
_____
_____

2) As we see in the chapter, the one thing we are to seek is to dwell in the Presence of the Lord. Have you battled desiring other things besides Christ or perhaps that are counter to Christ?

_____
_____
_____
_____
_____

3) As we see in the chapter, the Holy Spirit is described as the _Flame of Love_. What does this mean to you on a personal level?

_____
_____
_____
_____
_____

Additional thoughts:

_____

_____

_____

_____

_____

_____

_____

_____

_____

_____

_____

_____

_____

_____

4

THE ONE PEARL

Who, when he had found One Pearl of great price, went and sold all that he had, and bought it. (Matthew 13:46)

Each of us must seek this One Pearl, which is the Lord Jesus. But what we do with Him after we have found Him is the question of greatest importance, for Jesus Christ is forever the Pearl of the greatest value. To truly find Him requires all that you are and all that you have. Only with the eyes of your heart can Jesus, the Great Pearl, be seen, known, entered into, and esteemed. Only those who love Jesus with all their hearts, souls, minds, and strength will be purified in their hearts by the refining fire of Christ Jesus.

Our search for the One Great Pearl will come with trials and tribulations. We may find ourselves obstructed by many hindrances that attempt to deter us from our search. Yet, if our eyes remain fixed upon Him by His Spirit, His love will be found to be greater than all the issues of this life. Every distress in this life can and will be consoled by the burning love of the One Great Pearl. God has declared for all eternity that He is love. And for this reason, Jesus has created you and me. We were created by Him *for* Him. We were created by Him, to love Him. We were created for Him, that we might worship Him, love Him, and serve Him with all of our heart. Our true purpose in this life is to love Jesus with all our being. That is authentic discipleship.

Jesus Christ must occupy first place in our lives. It is essential that we have *first love* for Him, as we see in the book of Revelation, when Jesus addresses the church at Ephesus. (See Revelation 2:4.) When you encounter Christ's burning love, you realize that Jesus is a million times more valuable than all the other things of this world combined. When we encounter the Blood of His Cross by faith, we begin to enter into the fountains of the love of Jesus' heart, because His living waters, found in His Blood, will always bring forth life and light to our souls. As the song goes, "All the Blood of Jesus so precious, so powerful, so holy." Jesus' Cross is forever holy because it was adorned with Jesus Himself. Saturated with His own Blood, Jesus baptized the Cross, intended for criminals, with His Blood.

And as we seek the One Great Pearl, the one precious Pearl, the Lord Jesus Christ of Nazareth, we come closer to His intimate love. The closer we get to His intimate love, the more His intimate love will flood our hearts. When we begin to know the one true God, and Jesus Christ's love, He then becomes the first love in our lives. During every trial and tribulation, the Lord's love overcomes and floods it all. With His love, we shall know His Presence. We shall know His peace in the midst of storms.

We will know His first love, as He pours it into us. Now we return this love to Him, the only love He is worthy of receiving. There is a joy found in His love that is unspeakable. Jesus' love pierces all darkness. Jesus' love heals all sicknesses. I pray that every reader comprehends in their hearts the words found in this chapter. Those of you who treasure first love for Jesus will be the ones who live closer to Him. In that place, you shall be in the very intimacy of Heaven itself, every day. His divine love will be given this crown of life. My prayer is that you apprehend this: the gates of Heaven will not open to those who do not love the Lord with all their hearts, with all their souls, with all their minds, and with all their strength. This is the greatest of all the commandments. Jesus, by the arrows of His Spirit, desires to pierce our hearts with His love, every day. We only have one turn in this life. Jesus is waiting for our glance toward Him.

One glance of our eyes toward Jesus ravishes His heart!

So, saints, we must get this right. We must get it right today. Today is the day of our salvation. We must ask God to guard our hearts, and that, by the Holy Spirit, He will protect and continue to fan His blazing fire of love for us. Our eternal destiny rests upon the heart of Christ, for all the world.

Now, it is said that lurking around us in this life is another. As Scripture affirms, the enemy comes to steal, kill, and destroy. (See John 10:10.) He wants to steal, kill, and destroy your hunger, your thirst, your worship, and your love for Christ. His name is Satan. He is the father of lies and he will do all he can to see the flame of love in your heart quenched. Satan's desire is that your first love for Jesus will be extinguished so that you will redirect your affections to him. He'll do anything to lose your first love for God. He wants your affection. If the devil sees that your heart is not aflame with a first love for Jesus, he will probably not waste his time with you, since you pose no threat to his evil plans. You are like the rest of the world.

Church, we must realize that a lukewarm love for Jesus is what Satan desires. He knows that "so-called" Christians who have no burning first love for Jesus are victims of his evil, deceptive power. If the devil can deceive you and make you believe that you can live a life of halfhearted devotion for Jesus, he's

THE LOVE BOOK • 27

very content. Satan loves the hypocrisy of "religious love" for Jesus. What is "religious love"? It is saying you love Jesus while remaining absorbed with yourself. Religious love is being absorbed with your family, your career, your money, and with prestige in the affirmation of man. It's being absorbed with a selfish ambition and choosing sin over love for God. You must know that Jesus Christ is a jealous God. He is the Lover of your soul. Do you not know that Jesus is your Maker? That your Lord is your Maker? Your Maker is your Husband. Jesus, your Maker, is your Husband, and He cannot tolerate any rival for the affections of His bride.

His heart is grieved when your love for sin or self is greater than your love for Him. Therefore, there is only one way to the Great Pearl of Christ: the way of the Cross. The Cross is the place where you encounter Christ's divine love. This is the only way of knowing the one true God, and Jesus, whom He sent. There are those who are intimate with God and have become united in His love. They thirst and hunger for Him. Their one desire is Jesus. Their hearts are pure and they are not seeking God for selfish ambition or pride. Their hearts are aflame and united with the love of God's heart. Jesus' Cross, washed with His Blood, must be thrust forever into your hearts by the Spirit of God. In this, such a holy and pure love flows from your heart—from a heart that has been rent. Only then can you live a life that searches and hungers for ever greater intimacy with Jesus. Readers, my brethren, my friends, Jesus is the *One Pearl*.

There is no greater treasure to be found anywhere in all the uNIVerse than Jesus! This is my prayer for you; let us pray together:

Our Father, my Love, my Lord, my God, my King, let our passion forever compel us to You, all the days of our lives. May our passion compel us to make You, Jesus, the greatest desire of our lives. As Your Word declares, *"Let him kiss me with kisses of his mouth."* Let us be in complete oneness with our Beloved Lord Jesus, who is our final destination. For He is the One Great Pearl. The Lord Jesus Himself awaits His Beloved bride. Jesus, we know that Your love cost You everything. You asked nothing of us. While we were yet sinners, You died for us. You first drank of the cup of suffering. Jesus! You have eaten the honeycomb, and the honey in Your life is suffering. The honey is the sweetness of Your love that flows from Your heart forever. Amen.

CHAPTER FOUR
STUDY QUESTIONS

1) The search for the One Great Pearl will come with trials and tribulations, as the chapter states. What do those look like and how do you overcome them?

_____
_____
_____
_____
_____

2) The chapter says, "Now we return this love to Him, the only love He is worthy of receiving." What does his love look like and how is it different from mere human love?

_____
_____
_____
_____
_____

3) The chapter ends with a strong prayer. What does this prayer mean to you and how can it impact your life if prayed and lived out daily?

_____
_____
_____
_____
_____

Additional thoughts:

_____

_____

_____

_____

_____

_____

_____

_____

_____

_____

_____

_____

_____

_____

THE FLOOD GATES OF HIS HEART

What I'm about to share with you are revelations that God placed in my heart over a period of several nights many years ago. On December 31, 2012, this is what the Lord spoke to my heart:

I have not forgotten you. Greatness awaits you.

On January 1, 2013, New Year's Day, I wrote,

"The fruit of My Spirit is revealed in your life as a result of your intimacy with Me." The weight of the love that Jesus has for me is overwhelming. My heart faints for You, Jesus. In Your Presence, this is what I revealed to You. The weight of the love that Jesus has for me is overwhelming. My heart faints for You, Jesus, in Your Presence. This

is what I revealed to You, an overwhelming sense of my love. My heart literally throbbed and I wept. It lasted only for a brief moment.

There was a pure and absolute ecstasy that morning. Never had I experienced such an ecstasy in His holy Presence. The love of Jesus' Cross became so real to me. Jesus yearns to be yearned. I experienced the burning heart of Jesus. He is a burning fire, an all-consuming love. And then the Lord took me to the Song of Solomon. Let me share some of what that He placed in my heart from His Word. The Lord said, *"If you find My lover, what will you tell him? Tell him I faint for love for him. Turn your eyes towards Me."* He said, *"They overwhelm Me. Your eyes ravish Me. Just imagine that one glance of your eyes ravishes Me."* Just imagine, every time we think of Jesus during the day, the eyes of our heart ravish Him! What depth of His love. Jesus' Presence is absolutely everything. We must pursue Him. We must pursue His Presence.

As we read His Word in the Holy Scriptures, we must ask the Holy Spirit to reveal Jesus to our hearts. As we feast upon Scripture daily, we can encounter His Presence.

"Jesus has gifted me His heart. If I will give Him my heart, He opens His heart to me." These are the words that He spoke to my heart in my time

with Him this morning. The secret place is more than my prayer closet. The true secret place is Jesus' heart.

A couple of days later, at 5:00 a.m. on January 3, 2013, this was the revelation of the Holy Spirit in my heart:

I write; it is difficult for me to speak. I have felt such warmth, the warmth of God's precious Blood forgiving my sins. God allowed me quick access this morning to His abiding Presence. It was a time of resting and soaking in Him. Adoration from my Lord has filled my heart this morning. For some reason, the eyes of my heart were on the nailed feet of Jesus on the Cross. I could see His hands and I could see the hands of His mother reaching upward, trying to touch her Son's feet. She was touching and comforting her Son during His suffering by stroking His feet— feet that were nailed to the Cross, saturated in His own Blood. The pain of Jesus and His mother was so great. The pain that she had for her Son was overwhelming.

Then there were moments when I could feel Jesus' mother's heart as she held on to her Son's body. He was taken down from the Cross, as the pain and the grieving continued in my heart for some time. It was an overwhelming emotion deep inside my heart. There was an uncontrollable weeping, full of love. I am flooded with His love this morning, His love for me and my love for Him.

On May 14, 2013, the Holy Spirit inspired my heart to write:

I asked the Holy Spirit to take my heart into Heaven this morning. For a brief moment, I saw my heart on a beautiful, high mountain. There was a rushing waterfall flowing down from the peak of the mountain to a deep valley. Then the Spirit took me even higher, and there I saw a deep river flowing from a higher place on the higher mountain range, and in the background I saw a high mountain peak. Later, as I was resting in His Presence, I sense a quick lifting of my body upward. The true secret place, I have found, is the heart of our Lord Jesus Christ. He will give Himself to anyone who will diligently seek Him, to the one who comes with a first love for Him, and to the one who seeks His sacrificial love.

This is my prayer for all who read this book. I want you to know that there is no greater place than the divine place of the Presence of our Beloved Jesus Christ, the King of Glory. We must not come to Him for selfish gain or to merely gaze at Him from afar. He is so much more than a feeling or a manifestation. I pray that *The Love Book* will beckon you to the Lord, who waits to open the floodgates of His heart and release the living waters of His love into you.

CHAPTER FIVE

STUDY QUESTIONS

1) God spoke, "I have not forgotten you. Greatness awaits you." What sort of *greatness* is awaiting us as believers?

_____
_____
_____
_____
_____

2) "As we read His Word in the Holy Scriptures, we must ask the Holy Spirit to reveal Jesus to our hearts," is a direct quote from the chapter. What role does the Word of God play in our love walk?

_____
_____
_____
_____
_____

3) Have you found yourself observing Jesus from afar? What does it look like to bridge this gap and enter the floodgates of His heart?

_____
_____
_____
_____
_____

Additional thoughts:

_____

_____

_____

_____

_____

_____

_____

_____

_____

_____

_____

_____

_____

_____

_____

6

WHO IS A GOD LIKE YOU?

Who is a God like you, who pardons sin and
forgives the transgression of the remnant of his
inheritance? You do not stay angry forever but
delight to show mercy. (Micah 7:18 NIV)

What love can be found anywhere or in
anyone that could compare with God, who
pardons our iniquity? If there's anything that we have
learned from the Scriptures and the writings of
others, it's that we have a God who is unlike anyone
else, a God who pardons our iniquities. I've learned
from the Scriptures, as well as from the writings of
Mother Basilea Schlink, that Micah's words should
be the song of our heart. This is what she wrote: "Let
Micah's words be the song of our hearts. Who is a
God like you who pardon my iniquity?" It is said that
we should have a continual banner always raised

before our hearts. It should be in the shape of the Cross and read, "What God is like You, Jesus? What kind of God would leave Heaven?" Listen closely: *What kind of God would leave Heaven and willingly come to this earth to die for each one of us?*

That is why Mother Basilea Schlink asked this question: "When was the last time you cried out about your unrepentant sins?" That's a profound question. When was the last time any of us cried aloud about our unrepentant sin? I pray that, today, as you read *The Love Book*, your heart will be pierced by the Lord God's love. I pray by the Holy Spirit, that we will quiet our flesh and allow God to be God in our hearts. We must declare to the world that our precious and glorious Savior is waiting for the sound of our cries—namely, our cries over our sins. We must become nations of repentant people who are crying over their sin.

Yes, God's mercies are new every morning. Therefore, should we not arise every morning with hearts pierced by the lance of the love of Jesus Christ and His holy and exalted Blood? Listen to what was said: *God's mercies are new every morning.* Shouldn't we live every morning with hearts that are pierced by the lance of the love of Jesus Christ? I have read that we need to ponder certain issues: *Should I not express my love for God? Should I go to church today? Should I express my love for God by giving my tithe? Should I make the Lord first in my life?*

Today, we should be able to answer all these questions.

Yet, each day, we all should be singing the song: "What God is like You?" Let us sing that song with all our heart. "What God is like You, who pardons our iniquities?" I pray that through *The Love Book*, God is inspiring you to open your heart to the beautiful sound of that song. There's no one like our God. When you do, the Holy Spirit can shine forth in the depths of your hearts with a love that is unexplainable. His is a divine love from Heaven that will tear open your hearts. Let us cry out to the Holy Spirit, "Holy Spirit, tear open my heart, that You would illuminate the sins of my life." What contrition? What repentance will crush us? We must ask the Holy Spirit to open the secrets of our hearts.

We must give the Holy Spirit access to crush our hearts into a million pieces with His loving hands, that He may break us and destroy any semblance of self in our life. For this, we know by faith that our Father will take every broken piece of our hearts and place them in His holy hands. From there, in our Beloved Father's hands, the fountain of love will be poured out. He will press our brokenness and shape the pieces of our hearts into the image of His glorious Son, Jesus Christ! That is so beautiful!

Again, He will press the broken pieces and shape them into the image of His glorious Son, Jesus Christ of Nazareth. So, church, when we learn of God's love, the question must be asked, "Are we not to know repentance as well?" Repentance is not some grievous, difficult, harsh subject. I have read that "repentance is a holy call flowing from the joy of God's heart." I have also read that "repentance is God's holy gateway into the heart of Heaven." That's beautiful! Repentance is God's holy gateway into the heart of Heaven. For this reason, we must pray each day that God would keep us in brokenness, because then, Heaven will descend in power, His glory forever in our lives.

Do you seek Heaven's descent upon your life in power and glory? Then live in brokenness. We cannot know God's love unless we repent each day. How can we love God unless we cry out from our hearts, "Who is like You, Lord, who pardons my iniquities? There is no one like You, Jesus!" Have you ever read that all Heaven rejoices over one sinner who is *healed*? No. Have you ever read that that all Heaven rejoices when one sinner who is *saved from poverty*? No. But do we read that Heaven rejoices when *one sinner repents*? Yes. Only then does Heaven rejoice, when one sinner repents and comes unto salvation.

I have learned that we cannot know the godly fruit of the Lord in our lives unless we repent. You see, repentance and first love, repentance and bridal love, are forever linked. They are dependent on one another. So it is for the church to know that there is no access to the true Presence of God unless it be by the joy of repentance. I have learned that if I look at any heart that does not love God first, I am looking at a heart that does not sing the song, "Who is a God like You, that pardons iniquities?"

I have apprehended in my heart that bridal love is found in the one who comes to Jesus through the song of repentance. Now I want to speak directly to those followers of our Lord Jesus Christ. I say to you, let us once again come back to Jesus as never before. Let us come with rejoicing through hearts of repentance. Yes, once we too were prisoners to sin. There, we were hopeless. We were chained with no hope of escape, locked forever in darkness. It was a darkness of pain, of fear and death.

But our God, who is like no other god, came down willingly from Heaven and became one of us! Our God suffered and died because He chose to take our place on the Cross. He rose to life on the third day. Because of His love, we should sing praises unto Him and share with the whole world, "There's no other god like our God. There is no god like our God!" He alone rose from the grave and defeated death, hell, and the grave. Jesus alone gave us life through His precious and loving Blood. Because of Jesus Christ, we are free. Those of us who are free can never forget how we were once prisoners without hope. This is the beautiful love of God's heart.

This is why we cry out in repentance every day.

What Jesus Christ has done for us drives us to our knees. His love is so bright. True bridal love never forgets the love of Jesus Christ, our Beloved. It was Jesus who died; it was Jesus who suffered for the whole world, which includes you and me. I will always declare the love of His Cross, that it would be burned and branded upon every one of your hearts. Yes, Jesus is our song, and the Lord will always be our song. We will forever declare, "Who is like You, my God, who pardons my iniquities?"

Jesus, we give You all of our heart. We give You our soul and our body, that through our lives, You shall be declared to the whole world. I will declare by the Holy Spirit, and to all the world, of Your love, great power, and wondrous glory. "Your love, Your love, Jesus," is the song of our heart!

CHAPTER SIX

STUDY QUESTIONS

1) God endlessly loves people, as a result, He draws close and blesses the world. What is the purpose in God's blessing and what does it accomplish?

_____
_____
_____
_____
_____

2) Have you found yourself forgetting about God's unmatched love? What steps did you take to step back into the reality of His love?

_____
_____
_____
_____
_____

3) God's love is so great, is cannot be compared with any other. In what ways is His love greater than the mere human love we find on earth?

_____
_____
_____
_____
_____

Additional thoughts:

_____

_____

_____

_____

_____

_____

_____

_____

_____

_____

_____

_____

_____

_____

_____

OUR REST IS FOUND IN LOVING JESUS

G od has always had a plan to win your love. It is said, "The only resting place for any believer's faith is in loving Jesus Christ." Every thirsty soul will only find rest and satisfaction in loving Jesus. Once you have tasted the beauty and the goodness and the holiness and the power of Jesus' love, you can find satisfaction nowhere else. Satisfaction is found only in loving Jesus. You see, loving Jesus of Nazareth is the only place for the heart of a follower of Christ.

Jesus tells us in John 14:21, *"The one who loves me will be loved by my Father"* (NIV). The only place where you will find one walking in the perfected life is where one has a first love for Jesus. Your heart must be united with the heart of God. Our hearts must be united with the heart of the Lord Jesus. Such a love maintains a continual inti-

macy with God because our hearts remain united
with His first love. First love unites and preserves
intimacy with the Lord. It was St. Alphonsus de
Liguori who said, "Does not our God deserve such
love? Does He not deserve all of our love, who has
loved you us for all eternity?" God was the first to
ever love you.

> I in them and you in me—so that they may be
> brought to complete unity. Then the world will
> know that you sent me and have loved them even
> as you have loved me. Father, I want those you
> have given me to be with me where I am, and to
> see my glory, the glory you have given me
> because you loved me before the creation of the
> world. (John 17:23–24 NIV)

What does first love look like? The answer is
found in Jesus' Word. He loved us from the foundation of the world. Only God's love is a perfect love.
Only the Holy Spirit can enable perfect love to flow
out of our Father's heart and into our hearts. A
continual intimacy with God is a divine working of
the Holy Spirit, by which we become one with the
Father's perfect love. Since none of us can claim to
live in perfect love, it is only by the gift of repentance
that we approach God. Yes, daily, we all fall short of
God's glory and sin against Him. But His love is
perfect, illuminating our hopeless condition and then

restoring our hearts. His heart with our hearts —*bridal love*.

His perfect love restores His heart with our broken hearts. This is key, for in our brokenness, we are flooded with the perfect, loving forgiveness of God. It is repentance that enables God's grace of forgiveness. Let us never presume that since we were justified, we, from that point on, have no necessity to repent. That is a false gospel.

The repentant, broken heart opens us to be filled with God's forgiving, perfect love. Our lack of a life of repentance precludes deep intimacy. It becomes a hindrance. It becomes debris that continually inhibits our divine union with the Lord Jesus. Such an unforgiving heart is a heart of self-righteousness—and a heart of self-righteousness always grieves the Lord.

Such an unrepentant heart is a lukewarm heart. A self-righteous heart is a lukewarm heart, at the very least, for it is a heart that says, "I am rich and have no need of the grace of the Spirit of repentance." Such a heart shuts out the divine flow of God's perfect love. To be far away from our Beloved because of our self-sufficiency, or because of a lack of repentance or pride, destroys our spiritual life. The only way we can continue with the flow of God's love in our lives is by union with God, and through the love of repentance.

It is the flow of God's life within us that brings forth eternal life with Him. God gives us life to have life in Him. It's not our life; it's His life. When the prodigal son approached his father after wasting his inheritance through riotous living, he knelt down in contrition and repentance. It was that posture of the son's heart that compelled the overflowing of the father's love toward his son—repentance unto his father, and thus, unto God. The floodgates of God's love, and the grace of repentance, transformed the prodigal son's heart. His repentance gave birth to a new heart, a new life by the Holy Spirit—a life of love, peace, and joy.

My prayer is that as you read *The Love Book,* your heart, and the hearts of the entire church, will come before the Lord with same brokenness, contrition, and repentance. After such a sacred assembly of the heart, the Spirit of God will descend and be revealed. I pray the Kingdom of God will invade the hearts of people with His perfect love. God's love reigns in His Heavenly Kingdom. It is His love that causes hearts to rejoice with the name of Jesus Christ, in His Presence and with His power.

So, I close with these questions: *Where do we find first love? How is it found? How is it revealed in the church, where the bride lives in the place of selfless love?*

First love flows only from the heart of God. For it is His ultimate expression of love for you, which was revealed by Jesus Christ's death upon the Cross.

CHAPTER SEVEN
STUDY QUESTIONS

1) God's Presence is a resting place to us. Have you seen people who neglected this resting place? What was the result? How do we avoid this?

_____
_____
_____
_____
_____

2) It is said, "The only resting place for any believer's faith is in loving Jesus Christ." The Gospel is quite simple in this way. Why do we sometimes complicate it and what is the result of that?

_____
_____
_____
_____
_____

3) The chapter describes that we must come before the Lord in brokenness, contrition, and repentance. Practically speaking, what does this look like?

_____
_____
_____
_____
_____

Additional thoughts:

_____

_____

_____

_____

_____

_____

_____

_____

_____

_____

_____

_____

_____

_____

_____

_____

8

FIRST LOVE, GOD'S LOVE

The ultimate expression of God's love for all the world was Christ's death upon the Cross. To separate first love, bridal love, and God's divine love of His Cross is impossible. It is wrong to do so because the greatest love ever known, the greatest love ever beheld, was Jesus Christ—the loving, innocent, holy Lamb of God, who willingly gave Himself on the altar of His Cross. With every drop of His precious Blood that was shed—from the garden of Gethsemane to the halls of the high priests, from Pilate to the whipping post, from the sufferings on the Via Delorosa to the very Cross itself—love is revealed.

The shedding of Christ's Blood was a divine cry from God to all the world, "I love you!" This is why we must bring back the Cross and keep it before the eyes of our hearts. The resurrection came only because of His death upon the Cross. This is why William Penn said, "No Cross, no crown." It is for this reason that the Cross is always the mark of God's love for His bride, for His church, and for you and me. It is said, "There is nothing in Heaven that does not have the mark of the Cross upon it."

In Romans 5:8, the Scriptures declare that God has proven His love for you. He died for you while you were yet a sinner. There are many people in the church who *talk* about their first love for the Lord. But Jesus *affirmed* His first love. He proved everything He ever said or taught. He affirmed His love upon the Cross. God, who *is* love, chose to meet with Christ on either side of the Cross. God in Heaven, Jesus on earth, with the Cross separating them. It was on the Cross that love stretched forth one hand to you and the other to God the Father.

Jesus' hands were nailed to that Cross. His hands were divinely outstretched, one to the Father and the other to all who believe on Him. What good is our evangelism if we do not do the same? If we do not keep one hand forever stretched to the Father and the other to those in this world who are in need of the gospel, what good is it? Every time we lift up God, we're lifting up love. We are lifting up love from His Cross. His love draws all men to Himself and to His Cross. In Philippians 2:8, it says the Son of God chose to become obedient to death, even death on a Cross. Hear the cry of the love of Christ's heart. In

Psalm 22:14–15, He says, *"I am poured out like water, and all my bones are out of joint. My heart has turned to wax; it has melted within me. My mouth is dried up like a potsherd, and my tongue sticks to the roof of my mouth; you lay me in the dust of death"* (NIV).

Listen to His words and hear the cry of our Lord from His Cross. God, who *is* love, took on shame and was treated as the most vile criminal of all time. He became the accursed. His death was the confirmation of the Holy Spirit's words in John 3:16: *"For God so loved the world, that he gave his only begotten Son."* We must never forget those words. In John 10:11, God declares, *"The good shepherd lays down his life for the sheep"* (NIV). As Jesus hung upon the Cross, so great was His love that He would not allow His suffering to end quickly. He waited, out of His great love, experiencing the most agonizing suffering and pain ever known. Still, He waited until everything was finished and all had been fulfilled.

As we look at Jesus' life, His love compelled Him to lay down His life for your sake and mine. John the Baptist declared, *"Behold the Lamb of God, which taketh away the sin of the world"* (John 1:29). This is the Jesus who calls you with cords of love. This is true first love. This is the Jesus whom you say you seek and desire His Presence. You must seek and desire the Presence of the God of a Jesus who first went to the Cross. Even though we have removed His Cross, and Him crucified, from far too many church sanctuaries, He has not removed the memory of His love and His suffering. To this day, His hands, His feet, and His side continue to bear the scars of His love. This is true bridal love. This is true intimacy—to behold the Lamb of God, to behold your Husband. He said in His Word, "Do you not know your Maker is your Husband?" (See Isaiah 54:5.)

In Jesus, we find the true meaning of first love. Jesus is the One for whom you must hunger and thirst. He is the One for whom you must strive. He is the One who waits for you in the secret place of His heart. On the Cross, Jesus' Father turned away from Him for the first time in all eternity. But even as Jesus cried out, *"My God, my God, why hast thou forsaken me?"* (Matthew 27:46), Jesus' love for His Father, and the Father's love for His Son, never ceased. This was true love—even unto death.

Jesus' love was revealed in His own body upon the Cross. He was God's fragrant offering and sacrifice. His life was a fragrance that was offered and sacrificed. If we live by the Holy Spirit of Christ, should not our love have a substance to it as well? Should not first love be found in us as our lives are offered unto God as living sacrifices, holy and acceptable in His sight? A sacrifice is far more than just a casual offering. It is a sacrifice birthed out of great love. The Bible tells us that Christ died for sinners.

(See Romans 5:8.) This is the epitome of sacrificial love. Therein lies your greatest example of first love.

We speak of bridal love, a deeper revelation of *first love*. Bridal love is that intimate knowing of God. He has given all of His love for the entire world by the shedding of His Blood upon the Cross. His love for you looks like what He did. The Bible tells us that Jesus *"disarmed the powers and authorities, he made a public spectacle of them, triumphing over them by the Cross"* (Colossians 2:15 NIV). How do we triumph? We triumph in Christ, in His triumphant victory by way of His Cross.

Jesus is love. His love enables you to overcome. By way of the Blood of His Cross, Jesus Christ has given you the greatest example of what first love looks like. In divine love, as it was with Jesus, suffering is to be found. Insults will be found but never retaliated against. In first love, one makes no threats. In first love, you are totally entrusted. You've totally entrusted your life to God. In first love, Jesus bore our sins in His body on the tree. His love was revealed for all time upon the altar of His Cross, even as He was nailed to the tree as a criminal. His precious Blood carried His life. There, we witnessed true love. We find in His love a divine submission, a divine gentleness, meekness, and surrender. Isaiah 53:7 declares, *"He was oppressed and afflicted, yet he did not open his mouth"* (NIV).

He was led like a lamb to the slaughter. Romans

5:8 declares that God demonstrated His own love for us. He didn't merely talk about it; He gave His life. Everything Jesus proclaimed, He proved. No words could have been said that would equal the effect of what He did to prove His love on the Cross. The Cross was Jesus' pledge of His love for all the world —for all eternity. Every day that you carry your Cross, it's God's reminder of His love, and the responding pledge of your love for Him. First love is Christ's love. Christ's love compels us. In 2 Corinthians 5:14, Paul writes, *"Christ's love compels us.... And he died for all, that those who live should no longer live for themselves but for him who died for them and was raised again"* (NIV). The Cross will always be God's measure of divine love. It is also God's measure of our sin.

Jesus' Cross is the supreme act and proof of the love He has, and therefore, the love His Father has, for you. Jesus' love revealed upon His Cross was offered to the criminals hung on either side of Him. He offered each of them His love from the Cross. One of the criminals chose Jesus' love and received Him. The other rejected His love. Sadly, it is still the same today. There will be those who will receive Jesus' love and there will be those who reject His love. Some will become heirs of His love while others become the heirs of God's wrath. To reject Jesus' love, poured out from His Cross, is to reject God Himself, who sent Him to save the world.

1) We not only receive God's love but we reciprocate that love. What does *loving Him* look like to you?

_____
_____
_____
_____
_____

2) "How to" formulas can create an impersonal and merely transactional view of God. What other negative consequences come when one reduces God's love to a formula or method?

_____
_____
_____
_____
_____

3) The chapter talks about God's love being proven on the Cross of Jesus Christ. What happens when we feel that God needs to prove His love in other ways? How can this be damaging to our relationship with Him?

_____
_____
_____
_____
_____

Additional thoughts:

_____

_____

_____

_____

_____

_____

_____

_____

_____

_____

_____

_____

_____

_____

_____

_____

9

CONCLUSION

May I repeat myself by saying that *to reject Jesus' love, poured out upon His Cross, is to reject the God who sent Him to save the world*. In Song of Songs, we learn many beautiful truths. We also learn what must become the cry of our heart: "Lord Jesus, kiss me and kiss me again." (See Song of Songs 1:2.) The Lord's Presence is the sweetest and most precious fragrance there is. It is the Presence of the Lord Jesus that causes each of us to love Him. His love divinely draws us to love Him. We must not be timid to ask the Lord that He take us with Him, wherever He chooses. For we know that the King loves His bride. He desires to bring His bride into His chamber.

"My King," our hearts cry, "we praise Your love above anything else! Lord Jesus, it is only right that we, Your church, adore You. Jesus, we are Your bride.

Take Your bride with You wherever You go, wherever You choose to rest Your Presence. For where You go, Lord, Your bride desires to go. Jesus, look upon Your bride and declare, 'Most beautiful woman!' for the Lord's bride causes Him great excitement."

The Lord Jesus sees not the flaws of our lives. He sees only how lovely we are. He tells us in His Word that He sees His bride and His heart is set on fire, for Jesus declares He desires to adorn His bride with precious gold and silver. The King rests and meditates upon His bride and recollects the beauty of her fragrance. We learn in God's Word, over and over, that our King declares, *"How beautiful you are, my darling!"* (Song of Songs 4:1 NIV). We reply, "You are so handsome, my love. Your Presence pleases my soul."

Saints, beyond any words I can express, I pray that we, the bride of Christ, will seek to sit and to rest in the shade of the Presence of our Lord. It is the Holy Spirit who desires to escort our hearts to His banquet table, that He might prove how much the King loves His bride.

Lord, we are weak with our love for You. Your arms embrace us and hold us upright. Jesus, You are King. You are the Lover of our souls. We're so grateful that You look behind the walls of our hearts, so grateful that You peer into our hearts, as looking through a window. Every night and every morning,

You declare to our hearts, "Rise up, my darling, and come away with Me, My fair one." (See Song of Songs 2:10.) And our lover Jesus says, "Let Me see your face. Let Me hear your voice. For your voice is so pleasant to Me, and your face is so lovely." (See verse 14.) And let His bride declare, "My lover is mine and I am His." (See verse 16.) Jesus is ours and we are His. Yes, there will be nights when we will yearn for our Lord's Presence. There will be nights when we yearn for our Lord Jesus and He does not come. When He tarries, we will get up and roam the city, searching for Him.

We will search for the One whom we love. When we find our Beloved, and come into His Presence, we shall hold Him tightly and bring Him into the intimacy of our hearts. And when we do this by faith, Jesus will say, "You are beautiful, My darling—more beautiful than words. You are altogether beautiful, My darling. Come with Me, My bride. You have captured My heart. You are My treasure, My bride. One glance of your eyes ravishes My heart." (See Song of Songs 4:7–9).

CHAPTER NINE
STUDY QUESTIONS

1) The chapter states, "The Lord Jesus sees not the flaws of our lives. He sees only how lovely we are." How does this change the way you see yourself?

_____
_____
_____
_____
_____

2) The chapter talks about being embraced in the loving arms of Jesus. Have you experienced this? What does this feel like? What are the results of it on you, your personality, and your life as a whole?

_____
_____
_____
_____
_____

3) What testimonies can you recall either in your own life or the lives of others that stir up faith within you to pursue Jesus with everything you have?

_____
_____
_____
_____
_____

Additional thoughts:

_____
_____
_____
_____
_____

_____
_____
_____
_____
_____

_____
_____
_____
_____
_____

FINAL WORDS: THE HEART OF LOVE

There's a beautiful place of the heart that the truly devoted disciples of Christ Jesus will one day find. It's the revelation of the beauty of the gospel of Jesus Christ, the Cross, the Holy Spirit, the Blood of the Cross, the sweetness and the love of God Himself. For our Lord God is holy. He is our divine God, whom our hearts must always seek and desire. What is there of ourselves that the Holy Spirit of Christ Jesus does not know? Does He not know everything there is to know regarding our lives?

Jesus knows our infirmities. Not only the infirmities of our bodies but He also knows the infirmities of our souls. He knows the temptations that come before us and cause us to abandon our first love for God. He knows how we turn instead to our love for sin. Only God knows when, how, and why. Every follower of Christ is to be marked with divine scar tissue, which is our suffering for Jesus' namesake and our love for Him. And, of course, only the Comforter, the Holy Spirit of Christ, knows the weight of our burdens.

He is Holy God, who sees all of our lives. He sees our defiled hearts, and it is He alone who then will draw us back to beholding the Lamb of God, who was lifted up. The Holy Spirit is the One who wraps His cords of love around our hearts and draws us to Himself. Jesus Christ was stripped naked. He was made void of all earthly riches. He chose to be hung from the Cross, nailed to it with spikes driven into His holy body by evil men.

These were not just spikes of iron, made strong and sharp upon the burning coals of the blacksmith. These were spikes honed by the hands of evil and hatred and contempt and death. Yet the Father declares that He was pleased to crush His Son because of His great love for the world. Every day and every night, we must cry to our God for His mercy and grace. So that, by His loving Spirit, and by His precious Blood of the Cross, we may be one with God.

Every day of our lives, God looks to the Cross of His Son to find the broken heart and empty vessel. He looks to the Cross to find those whom He might fill with Himself. He pours blessings into those vessels who turn the eyes of their hearts to Him crucified. The committed disciple knows the reality of what dying to self truly entails. He or she knows that the more they forsake the things of this world for the sake of the Kingdom of Heaven, the sooner the grace of God's wind will be felt and known.

The goal of such a life with God is intimacy of oneness with our Beloved. It is an intimacy of harmony and unity perfected by the hands of God alone. It's for this reason that the true disciple abhors disunity, detests strife, envy, and pride, for all such evils hinder this oneness of divine intimacy with our Lord. There is a divine fire that is only found within the love of God's heart. And only this burning, refined, perfect love can illuminate the darkness of our souls. By the glorious light of His Presence, all of self is burned away. Every piece of the veil of our flesh that has kept us apart from the secret place of our Lord's heart is done away with. It is the Holy Spirit, each day within the loving heart of the disciple, who lifts him or her high upon the rock of God's salvation, which is the Lord Jesus Christ. Each day, the Spirit of Christ takes the disciple into the glorious splendor of Heaven itself.

The Lord Jesus' disciple is the one who cries out to be consumed in the fire of God's loving Presence. The disciple lives to be one with God in an unsurpassed holy union with the Lord, blended together by the melting of the heart of the disciple in the fire of His love. Some ask, "What does the disciple's love look like?" It is a love found within the heart of the one who is totally devoted to the divine love of the heart—the Lord God Himself. There, all the affections of the disciple burn only for the Lord. Did not David cry, *"One thing have I desired of the Lord, that will I seek after; that I may dwell in the house of the Lord all the days of my life, to behold the beauty of the Lord, and to enquire in his temple"* (Psalm 27:4)?

Church, this continues to this very day, and until the Lord's return. Let the voice of Jesus Christ be the cry of our hearts, as His disciples.

CHAPTER TEN
STUDY QUESTIONS

1) The chapter speaks of divine "scar tissue." What is this and what is its role in your life? Do you have "scar tissue" in your life?

_____
_____
_____
_____
_____

2) The Word repeatedly describes the blessings upon blessings that come to those who love Him. What sort of blessings have you seen in your own life as a result of loving Him?

_____
_____
_____
_____
_____

3) What happens when we lose sight of daily loving Jesus? Have you done this and what was the result? What are your "love goals" in moving forward?

_____
_____
_____
_____
_____

Additional thoughts:

_____

_____

_____

_____

_____

_____

_____

_____

_____

_____

_____

_____

_____

_____

_____

_____

Pastor Theo and his wife Evelyn, have spent the past nearly 30 years, revealing Jesus Christ by the power of the Holy Spirit, to both children and adults, throughout America, Brazil, Greece, Pakistan, India, the Philippines, and other parts of the world. They are the blessed parents of Theo and Michael Koulianos, and six grandchildren. They simply love Jesus with all their hearts and are devoted to seeing the name of the Lord spread abroad, in both word and deed. The Lord has been gracious to them, with His divine confirmation of signs, wonders, healings, and miracles following them; as they continue to this day in teaching the Kingdom of God, preaching the Gospel, and praying for the sick.

Discover more at:

⊕ JESUSCENTER.US

TO DISCOVER ADDITIONAL VOLUMES WITHIN THIS
GLOBAL DISCIPLESHIP COURSE, VISIT:

OR

TO CONNECT OR PARTNER WITH THE MINISTRY,
VISIT, CALL OR WRITE TO:

THE JESUS CENTER CHURCH

36750 US HWY 19 NORTH, STE 2051

PALM HARBOR, FLORIDA 34684

PHONE: (727) 412-1432

———

EMAIL:

GENERAL INFORMATION: *info@jesuscenter.us*

PASTOR THEO: *theo@jesuscenter.us*

EVELYN: *evelyn@jesuscenter.us*

SUGGESTED SCRIPTURE READING

20 PASSAGES ON LOVE

"For God so loved the world, that he gave his only begotten Son, that whosoever believeth in him should not perish, but have everlasting life."

(John 3:16)

"He that loveth not knoweth not God; for God is love."

(1 John 4:8)

"For I am persuaded, that neither death, nor life, nor angels, nor principalities, nor powers, nor things present, nor things to come, nor height, nor depth, nor any other creature, shall be able to separate us from the love of God, which is in Christ Jesus our Lord."

(Romans 8:38-39)

"A new commandment I give unto you, That ye love one another; as I have loved you, that ye also love one another."

(John 13:34)

"But God commendeth his love toward us, in that, while we were yet sinners, Christ died for us."

(Romans 5:8)

"Beloved, let us love one another: for love is of God; and every one that loveth is born of God, and knoweth God."

(1 John 4:7)

"I am crucified with Christ: nevertheless I live; yet not I, but Christ liveth in me: and the life which I now live in the flesh I live by the faith of the Son of God, who loved me, and gave himself for me."

(Galatians 2:20)

"And now abideth faith, hope, charity, these three; but the greatest of these [is] charity."

(1 Corinthians 13:13)

"Herein is love, not that we loved God, but that he loved us, and sent his Son [to be] the propitiation for our sins."

(1 John 4:10)

"Husbands, love your wives, even as Christ also loved the church, and gave himself for it…"

(Ephesians 5:25)

"Greater love hath no man than this, that a man lay down his life for his friends."

(John 15:13)

"The LORD hath appeared of old unto me, [saying], Yea, I have loved thee with an everlasting love: therefore with lovingkindness have I drawn thee."

(Jeremiah 31:3)

"For this is the love of God, that we keep his commandments: and his commandments are not grievous."

(1 John 5:3)

"Cause me to hear thy lovingkindness in the morning; for in thee do I trust: cause me to know the way wherein I should walk; for I lift up my soul unto thee."

(Psalm 143:8)

"And above all these things put on [love], which is the bond of perfectness."

(Colossians 3:14)

"And we have known and believed the love that God hath to us. God is love; and he that dwelleth in love dwelleth in God, and God in him."

(1 John 4:16)

"We love him, because he first loved us."

(1 John 4:19)

"And now abideth faith, hope, [love], these three; but the greatest of these is [love]."

(1 Corinthians 13:13)

"And above all things have fervent charity among your-selves: for [love] shall cover the multitude of sins."

(1 Peter 4:8)

"This is my commandment, That ye love one another, as I have loved you."

(John 15:12)

NOTES

Made in the USA
Las Vegas, NV
29 October 2021

33295594R00059